Luxembourg

Everything You Need to Know

4

Introduction to Luxembourg

Nestled in the heart of Europe, Luxembourg stands as a testament to the coexistence of rich history, modernity, and natural beauty. Despite its modest size, this landlocked country holds immense significance, both culturally and economically. Bordered by Belgium, France, and Germany, Luxembourg is strategically positioned, often referred to as the "crossroads of Europe."

With a land area spanning approximately 2,586 square kilometers (998 square miles), Luxembourg is one of the smallest sovereign states in Europe. Yet, its diminutive size belies its influence, particularly in the realms of finance and politics. The Grand Duchy of Luxembourg, as it is officially known, is a constitutional monarchy with a parliamentary democracy, with the Grand Duke serving as the head of state and a Prime Minister heading the government.

The origins of Luxembourg trace back to ancient times, with evidence of human habitation dating back to the Roman era. Over the centuries, it evolved from a medieval fortress to a thriving city-state and eventually to a modern European nation. Its strategic location has made it a prized possession throughout history, leading to numerous conflicts and changes in rulership.

Luxembourg City, the capital and largest city of the country, is a UNESCO World Heritage Site, renowned for its picturesque old town and impressive fortifications. The city's strategic location atop rocky cliffs overlooking the Alzette and Pétrusse rivers made it an ideal spot for fortresses, earning it the nickname "Gibraltar of the North."

Beyond its urban centers, Luxembourg boasts a diverse landscape characterized by rolling hills, dense forests, and meandering rivers. The Ardennes region in the north offers breathtaking vistas and outdoor recreational opportunities, while the Müllerthal region, often dubbed the "Little Switzerland of Luxembourg," captivates visitors with its stunning rock formations and winding trails.

Luxembourg's linguistic landscape is equally fascinating, with Luxembourgish, French, and German recognized as official languages. Luxembourgish, a Germanic language with French and Latin influences, serves as the national language and is widely spoken in everyday life, alongside French and German, which are commonly used in administration, business, and education.

Economically, Luxembourg punches above its weight, with a highly developed and diverse economy driven by finance, technology, and services. Home to numerous multinational corporations, including major players in the banking and investment sectors, Luxembourg is often regarded as a global financial hub.

In addition to its economic prowess, Luxembourg prides itself on its commitment to multiculturalism, social cohesion, and environmental sustainability. The country's high standard of living, coupled with its excellent healthcare and education systems, makes it an attractive destination for both residents and expatriates alike.

As we embark on this journey to explore everything Luxembourg has to offer, let us delve deeper into its rich tapestry of history, culture, and natural wonders, uncovering the hidden gems that make this small yet mighty nation a truly remarkable destination.

Geography and Landscape

Luxembourg, though small in size, boasts a diverse and captivating geography that encompasses a variety of landscapes, from lush forests to rolling hills and winding rivers. Situated in Western Europe, Luxembourg is landlocked and bordered by Belgium to the west, France to the south, and Germany to the east and north. With a total land area of approximately 2,586 square kilometers (998 square miles), it is one of the smallest countries in Europe.

The country's terrain is predominantly characterized by the Ardennes region in the north and the Gutland region in the south. The Ardennes, occupying about one-third of Luxembourg's territory, features picturesque hills, dense forests, and charming villages. This region is known for its natural beauty and is a popular destination for outdoor activities such as hiking, cycling, and wildlife observation.

The Müllerthal region, often referred to as "Little Switzerland" due to its stunning resemblance to the Swiss landscape, is located in the eastern part of Luxembourg. Here, visitors can explore dramatic rock formations, cascading waterfalls, and winding trails that meander through lush greenery. The Müllerthal Trail, a 112-kilometer (70-mile) long hiking route, offers breathtaking views and opportunities for adventure seekers.

In contrast to the rugged terrain of the Ardennes and Müllerthal, the Gutland region in the south of

Luxembourg is characterized by gently rolling hills, fertile valleys, and picturesque vineyards. This area is home to much of Luxembourg's agricultural land, producing a variety of crops, including grapes for wine production.

Luxembourg is crisscrossed by several rivers, the most significant of which are the Alzette, the Pétrusse, and the Sûre. These waterways not only contribute to the country's natural beauty but also play a vital role in its ecosystem and economy. The Alzette River flows through Luxembourg City, dividing the capital into distinct neighborhoods and contributing to its scenic charm.

Despite its relatively small size, Luxembourg is blessed with abundant green spaces and protected areas, including nature reserves, parks, and forests. These areas serve as important habitats for a diverse range of flora and fauna, including rare and endangered species.

Overall, Luxembourg's geography and landscape offer a delightful blend of natural beauty, cultural heritage, and outdoor recreational opportunities, making it a destination worth exploring for nature enthusiasts and adventure seekers alike.

Historical Overview: From Ancient Times to Present

Embark on a journey through time as we uncover the rich historical tapestry of Luxembourg, tracing its roots from ancient times to the present day. The story of Luxembourg is one of resilience, adaptation, and transformation, shaped by centuries of political intrigue, territorial disputes, and cultural exchanges.

The earliest evidence of human habitation in the region dates back to the Paleolithic era, with archaeological finds suggesting that ancient peoples inhabited the area as early as 35,000 years ago. Over the millennia, various Celtic tribes, including the Treveri and the Celts, settled in the region, leaving behind traces of their presence in the form of artifacts and settlements.

In the first century BCE, the Romans conquered the area and established a fortified settlement known as "Lucilinburhuc," which served as a strategic outpost along the Roman road network. The Roman influence can still be seen today in the form of archaeological sites and Roman artifacts scattered throughout the country.

Following the decline of the Roman Empire, Luxembourg became part of the Frankish Empire under the rule of Charlemagne. It was during this time that the foundations of modern Luxembourg were laid, with the emergence of fortified castles and the establishment of feudal domains.

In the Middle Ages, Luxembourg flourished as a prosperous trading hub and seat of power for noble families such as the House of Luxembourg. The construction of fortified castles, including the iconic Castle of Luxembourg, played a crucial role in defending the territory and asserting its sovereignty.

The 14th and 15th centuries saw Luxembourg emerge as a powerful duchy under the rule of the House of Luxembourg, with the coronation of Emperor Charles IV as Holy Roman Emperor solidifying its status as a prominent European power.

However, Luxembourg's fortunes took a downturn in the ensuing centuries, as it became embroiled in conflicts and power struggles with neighboring territories. The Treaty of London in 1867 guaranteed Luxembourg's independence and neutrality, paving the way for its transformation into a modern constitutional monarchy.

Luxembourg played a pivotal role in European politics during the 20th century, serving as a founding member of the European Union and hosting key institutions such as the European Court of Justice and the European Investment Bank. Today, Luxembourg stands as a testament to the resilience and adaptability of its people, embodying the spirit of unity and cooperation that defines modern Europe.

The Founding of Luxembourg City

In the annals of Luxembourg's history, the founding of its capital city, Luxembourg City, stands as a pivotal moment, marking the birth of a settlement that would grow to become a significant European hub. The origins of Luxembourg City trace back to the Roman era when a fortified outpost known as "Lucilinburhuc" was established atop a rocky plateau overlooking the Alzette and Pétrusse rivers. This strategic location provided a natural defense against potential invaders and facilitated trade along the Roman road network.

During the Middle Ages, Luxembourg City flourished as a center of commerce and governance, thanks in part to its advantageous position along key trade routes. The construction of imposing fortifications, including the iconic Casemates du Bock, further solidified the city's defensive capabilities and symbolized its status as a bastion of power in the region.

In the 10th century, Count Siegfried of Ardennes laid the foundations for the city's future prosperity by building a fortified castle on the site of the former Roman outpost. This castle, known as the Castle of Luxembourg, served as the seat of the ruling House of Luxembourg and played a crucial role in shaping the city's identity and development.

Over the centuries, Luxembourg City grew in importance as a political, economic, and cultural center, attracting merchants, artisans, and scholars from across Europe. The city's strategic position at the crossroads of major trade routes contributed to its prosperity, while its impressive fortifications and strategic alliances ensured its survival amidst the turmoil of medieval warfare and dynastic struggles.

In the 14th and 15th centuries, Luxembourg City reached its zenith under the rule of the House of Luxembourg, with the coronation of Emperor Charles IV as Holy Roman Emperor solidifying its status as a prominent European power. The city's prosperity was further enhanced by the flourishing of trade and the arts, as evidenced by the construction of magnificent Gothic cathedrals and the patronage of renowned artists and architects.

Despite periods of conflict and occupation, including during the Burgundian Wars and the Thirty Years' War, Luxembourg City endured and continued to thrive as a center of commerce, culture, and diplomacy. The Treaty of London in 1867, which guaranteed Luxembourg's independence and neutrality, marked a new chapter in the city's history, paving the way for its transformation into a modern European capital.

Today, Luxembourg City stands as a vibrant metropolis that seamlessly blends its rich historical heritage with modernity. Its picturesque old town, stunning architecture, and cosmopolitan atmosphere make it a popular destination for visitors from around the world, while its role as a global financial center and seat of European institutions underscores its continued relevance on the international stage.

Medieval Luxembourg: Castles and Fortifications

In the medieval period, Luxembourg emerged as a formidable stronghold, boasting a network of castles and fortifications that served to defend its territory and assert its sovereignty. At the heart of this defensive system stood the Castle of Luxembourg, perched atop a rocky plateau overlooking the Alzette and Pétrusse rivers. Built in the 10th century by Count Siegfried of Ardennes, this imposing fortress became the seat of the ruling House of Luxembourg and played a crucial role in shaping the city's identity and development.

In addition to the Castle of Luxembourg, the city was surrounded by a series of fortified walls and ramparts, which provided further protection against potential invaders. These walls were strengthened over time, particularly during the 14th and 15th centuries, as the city grew in importance as a political, economic, and cultural center. The construction of bastions, towers, and gatehouses enhanced the city's defensive capabilities and symbolized its status as a bastion of power in the region.

One of the most iconic features of medieval Luxembourg City was the Casemates du Bock, a network of underground passages and chambers carved into the rock beneath the fortress. Originally built as a defensive measure to provide shelter for soldiers and supplies during sieges, the Casemates du Bock later served as a refuge for the city's inhabitants during times of conflict. Today, this UNESCO World Heritage Site offers visitors a glimpse into the city's medieval past and its strategic importance as a military stronghold.

Beyond Luxembourg City, medieval Luxembourg was dotted with numerous castles and fortifications, each with its own unique history and significance. These castles served as both defensive structures and symbols of feudal power, with many built atop strategic hilltops or along key trade routes. Examples include the Castle of Vianden, a majestic fortress overlooking the Our River valley, and the Castle of Larochette, perched atop a rocky promontory in the Müllerthal region.

Throughout the medieval period, Luxembourg's castles and fortifications played a crucial role in defending the territory against external threats and asserting the authority of its rulers. While many of these structures fell into disrepair or were destroyed over the centuries, their legacy lives on in the form of ruins, archaeological sites, and restored monuments that dot the landscape of modern Luxembourg.

Modern History: Wars, Treaties, and Sovereignty

As we delve into the modern history of Luxembourg, we uncover a tapestry woven with threads of wars, treaties, and struggles for sovereignty. The 19th and 20th centuries were particularly tumultuous for this small European nation, marked by periods of conflict, occupation, and political upheaval.

The 19th century ushered in a wave of change for Luxembourg, as the Congress of Vienna in 1815 resulted in the country's inclusion in the German Confederation under the rule of the Dutch House of Orange-Nassau. However, Luxembourg's sovereignty was challenged in 1839 when the Treaty of London granted Belgium its independence, dividing the Grand Duchy of Luxembourg and sparking tensions between European powers.

Luxembourg's strategic location and valuable resources made it a coveted prize during the Franco-Prussian War of 1870-1871. The Treaty of London in 1867 had declared Luxembourg's perpetual neutrality, yet this did not prevent Prussian forces from occupying the country and incorporating it into the newly formed German Empire.

Following the conclusion of World War I, Luxembourg regained its independence and sovereignty, thanks in part to the Treaty of Versailles in 1919. The country emerged from the conflict relatively unscathed but faced economic challenges and political instability in the aftermath of the war.

Luxembourg's fortunes took a darker turn with the outbreak of World War II, as Nazi Germany invaded and occupied the country in 1940. Despite resistance efforts and acts of defiance, Luxembourg endured nearly five years of Nazi rule before Allied forces liberated the country in 1944-1945.

In the post-war period, Luxembourg emerged as a staunch advocate for European unity and cooperation, playing a key role in the founding of the European Coal and Steel Community (ECSC) in 1951. This initiative laid the groundwork for the European Union (EU) and positioned Luxembourg as a leading voice in European politics and diplomacy.

Luxembourg's commitment to international cooperation was further demonstrated by its role as a founding member of NATO in 1949 and its active participation in global peacekeeping missions and humanitarian efforts.

Throughout the latter half of the 20th century and into the 21st century, Luxembourg has continued to navigate the complexities of modern geopolitics while upholding its values of democracy, neutrality, and multilateralism. Today, the Grand Duchy of Luxembourg stands as a testament to the resilience and determination of its people, embodying the spirit of European unity and solidarity.

Luxembourg's Role in European Politics

Luxembourg, despite its small size, has played a significant role in shaping European politics and governance. As one of the six founding members of the European Coal and Steel Community (ECSC) in 1951, Luxembourg laid the foundation for what would later evolve into the European Union (EU). This initiative, aimed at fostering economic cooperation and preventing future conflicts, underscored Luxembourg's commitment to regional stability and prosperity.

Over the years, Luxembourg has actively participated in the integration process of the EU, contributing to the development of common policies and institutions. The country's leaders have been vocal advocates for deeper European integration, emphasizing the importance of solidarity, cooperation, and shared values among member states.

Luxembourg's role in European politics extends beyond its participation in EU institutions. The city of Luxembourg serves as the official seat of several key EU institutions, including the European Court of Justice, the European Court of Auditors, and parts of the European Investment Bank. This presence has solidified Luxembourg's status as a hub for European governance and jurisprudence.

Furthermore, Luxembourg has been a strong supporter of European initiatives aimed at promoting peace, security, and human rights. The country has contributed troops to various EU-led peacekeeping missions and has been an active participant in efforts to address global challenges such as climate change, migration, and terrorism.

In addition to its involvement in EU affairs, Luxembourg has also played a role in shaping international diplomacy and cooperation. The country has served multiple terms on the United Nations Security Council and has been a vocal advocate for multilateralism and diplomacy as a means of resolving conflicts and advancing global peace and stability.

Luxembourg's commitment to European values and principles is reflected in its domestic policies as well. The country has prioritized social welfare, education, and healthcare, ensuring a high quality of life for its citizens and residents. This commitment to social cohesion and solidarity aligns with the broader objectives of the EU and underscores Luxembourg's role as a progressive and forward-thinking member state.

In conclusion, Luxembourg's role in European politics is characterized by its active participation in EU institutions, its support for regional integration and cooperation, and its commitment to promoting peace, security, and human rights on the international stage. As a small yet influential player in European affairs, Luxembourg continues to contribute to the shaping of a more united and prosperous Europe.

The Grand Duchy of Luxembourg: Government and Institutions

In the Grand Duchy of Luxembourg, governance and institutions are shaped by a system of constitutional monarchy and parliamentary democracy. At the head of state sits the Grand Duke, currently Grand Duke Henri, who exercises ceremonial duties and represents the nation both domestically and internationally. While the Grand Duke holds symbolic significance, executive power is vested in the government, led by the Prime Minister.

Luxembourg operates under a multi-party system, with political power distributed among various political parties. The Chamber of Deputies, the country's unicameral legislative body, consists of 60 members elected by proportional representation for five-year terms. These deputies represent the interests of Luxembourg's diverse population and are responsible for passing laws, approving budgets, and overseeing government actions.

The government of Luxembourg operates within the framework of the Constitution of Luxembourg, which was adopted in 1868 and has since been amended to reflect the evolving needs and values of the nation. The Constitution delineates the powers and responsibilities of the different branches of government, as well as the rights and freedoms of citizens.

In addition to the Chamber of Deputies, Luxembourg's political landscape includes the Council of State, an advisory body composed of 21 members appointed by the Grand Duke. The Council of State provides legal advice to the government and reviews draft legislation before it is presented to the Chamber of Deputies for consideration.

The judiciary in Luxembourg is independent and impartial, ensuring the rule of law and protecting the rights of individuals. The judicial system is composed of various courts, including district courts, higher courts, and the Court of Cassation, which serves as the highest court of appeal in the country. Luxembourg is also home to the European Court of Justice, which interprets EU law and ensures its uniform application throughout the EU member states.

In addition to its domestic institutions, Luxembourg actively participates in international organizations and initiatives, including the United Nations, the European Union, and NATO. The country is known for its commitment to multilateralism, diplomacy, and humanitarian aid, and it plays an active role in promoting peace, security, and sustainable development on the global stage.

Overall, the government and institutions of the Grand Duchy of Luxembourg reflect a commitment to democracy, the rule of law, and respect for human rights. Through a system of checks and balances, political pluralism, and civic engagement, Luxembourg seeks to uphold the principles of good governance and ensure the well-being and prosperity of its citizens.

Economy and Finance: Banking and Business

When it comes to the economy and finance, Luxembourg punches above its weight. Renowned for its robust banking sector and favorable business environment, the Grand Duchy has established itself as a global financial hub. The roots of Luxembourg's financial prowess can be traced back to the early 20th century when the country enacted laws to attract foreign investment and capital. Today, Luxembourg is home to over 140 banks, including major international institutions and private banks. The country's banking sector is known for its stability, confidentiality, and expertise in wealth management and investment banking.

In addition to banking, Luxembourg has diversified its economy through various industries, including finance, technology, logistics, and manufacturing. The country's strategic location at the heart of Europe, coupled with its well-developed infrastructure and skilled workforce, has made it an attractive destination for multinational corporations and startups alike. Luxembourg's business-friendly policies, low corporate tax rates, and access to EU markets have further bolstered its appeal as a business hub.

The financial services industry is a key driver of Luxembourg's economy, accounting for a significant portion of its GDP and employment. The country's status as a leading global center for investment funds, insurance, and asset management has earned it the nickname "the fund center of Europe." Luxembourg is home to over 4,000 investment funds, with assets under management exceeding €4 trillion.

Luxembourg's success as a financial center is underpinned by its regulatory framework, which adheres to international standards and promotes transparency, integrity, and investor protection. The country's financial regulator, the Commission de Surveillance du Secteur Financier (CSSF), oversees the banking and financial services sector, ensuring compliance with regulations and safeguarding the stability of the financial system.

In recent years, Luxembourg has also emerged as a leader in sustainable finance and green investment. The country has introduced initiatives to promote environmental, social, and governance (ESG) principles in finance, including the issuance of green bonds and the development of sustainable investment products. Luxembourg is committed to becoming a global leader in sustainable finance, leveraging its expertise and resources to address pressing environmental and social challenges.

Overall, Luxembourg's economy and finance sector continue to thrive, driven by innovation, diversification, and a commitment to excellence. As the country looks to the future, it remains well-positioned to capitalize on emerging opportunities and maintain its status as a dynamic and resilient economic powerhouse.

Luxembourg's Multilingual Identity

Luxembourg's multilingual identity is as rich and diverse as its cultural heritage. Situated at the crossroads of Europe, the Grand Duchy is home to three official languages: Luxembourgish, French, and German. This linguistic diversity reflects the country's unique historical and geographical context, shaped by centuries of influence from neighboring regions.

Luxembourgish, a Germanic language with French and Latin influences, serves as the national language and is spoken by the majority of the population. It is the language of everyday communication, used in informal settings, at home, and among friends and family. Luxembourgish is also taught in schools and is an integral part of the nation's cultural identity, celebrated through literature, music, and media.

French is widely used in administration, business, and education, reflecting Luxembourg's close ties to its French-speaking neighbors. It is the primary language of government and official documents, as well as the preferred language of instruction in many schools and universities. French is also commonly spoken in professional settings, particularly in the banking and finance sectors, where it serves as a lingua franca among international professionals.

German, another official language of Luxembourg, holds significance in both historical and cultural contexts. It is taught in schools alongside Luxembourgish and French and is widely understood by the population. German-language media and literature also play a role in shaping Luxembourg's cultural landscape, contributing to the country's multilingual identity.

In addition to Luxembourgish, French, and German, English is increasingly spoken and understood in Luxembourg, particularly among younger generations and in international business circles. English-language education is widely available, and many Luxembourgish citizens are fluent in English, making it a valuable asset in the globalized world.

Luxembourg's multilingualism is not only a reflection of its diverse linguistic heritage but also a source of strength and unity. The ability to communicate in multiple languages fosters cross-cultural understanding, facilitates international cooperation, and enhances opportunities for economic and social mobility. It is a testament to Luxembourg's commitment to inclusivity, diversity, and openness to the world.

In conclusion, Luxembourg's multilingual identity is a defining feature of its national character, rooted in history, culture, and geography. The coexistence of Luxembourgish, French, German, and English languages enriches the country's social fabric, strengthens its international standing, and exemplifies the spirit of unity in diversity.

Luxembourgish Language and its Importance

The Luxembourgish language holds a special place in the hearts of Luxembourgers, serving as a cornerstone of their national identity. As a Germanic language with French and Latin influences, Luxembourgish is unique in its linguistic characteristics and reflects the country's rich cultural heritage. While Luxembourgish is not widely spoken outside of Luxembourg, it is the primary language of communication among the local population.

Despite its relatively small number of speakers, Luxembourgish plays a crucial role in everyday life, serving as the language of informal communication, family gatherings, and social interactions. It is the language in which children first learn to speak and express themselves, instilling a sense of belonging and cultural pride from an early age. Luxembourgish is also used in literature, poetry, music, and theater, contributing to the preservation and promotion of the language.

In recent years, efforts have been made to elevate the status of Luxembourgish and promote its use in official contexts. In 1984, Luxembourgish was recognized as an official language of the Grand Duchy, alongside French and German. Since then, steps have been taken to integrate Luxembourgish into education, administration, and media, ensuring its continued relevance and vitality.

Luxembourgish language instruction is now offered in schools, with a focus on promoting bilingualism and multilingualism among students. Additionally, Luxembourgish language courses are available for adults, immigrants, and expatriates, providing opportunities for language acquisition and cultural integration.

The importance of Luxembourgish extends beyond linguistic considerations. It serves as a symbol of national unity and solidarity, bridging cultural and regional differences among Luxembourgers. In a country where multiculturalism is celebrated, Luxembourgish acts as a common thread that binds the diverse communities together, fostering a sense of community and belonging.

Moreover, Luxembourgish plays a practical role in facilitating communication and fostering social cohesion within the country. It allows Luxembourgers to connect with one another on a deeper level, fostering empathy, understanding, and mutual respect across linguistic and cultural boundaries.

In conclusion, the Luxembourgish language holds significant cultural, social, and symbolic importance in the Grand Duchy of Luxembourg. It is a reflection of the country's rich heritage and a source of pride for its people. As efforts to promote and preserve Luxembourgish continue, the language will remain a vital aspect of Luxembourg's identity and cultural landscape for generations to come.

Cultural Diversity: Traditions and Festivals

Luxembourg's cultural landscape is as diverse as its linguistic heritage, reflecting a blend of influences from neighboring regions and beyond. The Grand Duchy boasts a rich tapestry of traditions, customs, and festivals that celebrate its multicultural identity and historical roots.

One of the most iconic cultural traditions in Luxembourg is the celebration of Carnival, known locally as "Fuesend." This festive season, which typically takes place in February, is marked by colorful parades, elaborate costumes, and lively street parties. Carnival festivities vary from region to region, with each community putting its own unique spin on the tradition.

Religious holidays also play a significant role in Luxembourg's cultural calendar, with Christmas and Easter being among the most widely celebrated. During the Christmas season, cities and towns are adorned with festive decorations, Christmas markets spring up in town squares, and traditional Christmas dishes like "Gromperekichelcher" (potato pancakes) are enjoyed by families and friends. Easter is celebrated with religious services, family gatherings, and the traditional Easter egg hunt.

Luxembourg's culinary heritage is another cornerstone of its cultural identity, with a diverse array of dishes and delicacies reflecting its multicultural influences. From hearty dishes like "Judd mat Gaardebounen" (smoked pork collar with broad beans) to sweet treats like "Quetschentaart" (plum tart), Luxembourg's cuisine is a testament to its rich culinary tradition.

In addition to traditional customs and culinary delights, Luxembourg also boasts a vibrant arts and music scene. The country is home to numerous theaters, galleries, and concert halls, where both local and international artists showcase their talents. Luxembourg's music festivals, such as the Echternach International Music Festival and the Rock um Knuedler, draw crowds of music enthusiasts from near and far.

Furthermore, Luxembourg's cultural diversity is reflected in its museums and cultural institutions, which showcase the country's history, art, and heritage. The National Museum of History and Art, the Mudam (Museum of Modern Art), and the Luxembourg City History Museum are just a few examples of the cultural treasures waiting to be discovered.

Throughout the year, Luxembourg hosts a variety of cultural events and festivals that celebrate its diverse heritage and foster cultural exchange. Whether it's the Schueberfouer, a centuries-old fair held in Luxembourg City, or the Octave Pilgrimage in the town of Luxembourg, these events bring communities together and showcase the best of Luxembourg's cultural traditions.

In essence, Luxembourg's cultural diversity is a source of pride and inspiration, enriching the fabric of society and strengthening bonds among its people. From centuries-old traditions to contemporary artistic expressions, Luxembourg's cultural landscape is a vibrant tapestry that continues to evolve and thrive.

Luxembourgian Cuisine: From Gromperekichelcher to Rieslingspaschtéit

Luxembourgian cuisine is a delightful fusion of flavors and influences, reflecting the country's rich culinary heritage and multicultural identity. From hearty traditional dishes to gourmet delicacies, Luxembourgian cuisine offers something to tantalize every palate.

One of the most beloved Luxembourgian dishes is Gromperekichelcher, a mouthwatering treat made from grated potatoes, onions, and herbs, formed into patties and fried until golden brown. These crispy potato pancakes are a favorite snack or appetizer, often served with applesauce or accompanied by a refreshing local beer.

Another iconic Luxembourgian dish is Judd mat Gaardebounen, featuring smoked pork collar cooked with broad beans in a savory broth. This hearty and comforting dish is a staple of Luxembourgian cuisine, particularly during the colder months, and is often served with boiled potatoes or crusty bread.

Rieslingspaschtéit, or Riesling pie, is a classic Luxembourgian dish that showcases the country's love for pastry and wine. This savory pie is filled with tender pieces of pork, vegetables, and aromatic herbs, all simmered in a flavorful Riesling wine sauce. The pie is then encased in a flaky pastry crust and baked to golden perfection, resulting in a deliciously satisfying meal.

Luxembourgian cuisine also boasts a variety of sweet treats and desserts, including Quetschentaart, a traditional plum tart made with juicy plums, almond filling, and a buttery pastry crust. This indulgent dessert is a popular choice for special occasions and family gatherings, often enjoyed with a dollop of whipped cream or a scoop of vanilla ice cream.

In addition to these iconic dishes, Luxembourgian cuisine is also influenced by its neighboring countries, with flavors and ingredients borrowed from French, German, and Belgian culinary traditions. Luxembourg's multicultural population has contributed to a vibrant food scene, with a wide range of international cuisines represented in restaurants and eateries across the country.

Luxembourg's wine culture is also worth mentioning, with the country's Moselle region producing high-quality white wines, including Riesling, Pinot Blanc, and Auxerrois. Wine tasting tours and vineyard visits are popular activities for locals and visitors alike, offering the chance to sample some of Luxembourg's finest vintages while enjoying the picturesque scenery of the Moselle Valley.

Overall, Luxembourgian cuisine is a celebration of flavors, traditions, and culinary craftsmanship. Whether you're savoring a hearty potato pancake, indulging in a savory meat pie, or enjoying a glass of crisp Riesling wine, Luxembourg's culinary delights are sure to leave a lasting impression on your taste buds.

Fine Dining and Culinary Delights

Luxembourg offers a delightful array of fine dining experiences and culinary delights that cater to every taste and preference. In the heart of Luxembourg City and beyond, you'll find a diverse range of restaurants, bistros, and eateries that showcase the country's culinary prowess and commitment to gastronomic excellence. From Michelin-starred establishments to cozy neighborhood cafes, Luxembourg's dining scene has something to offer for every occasion and palate.

Michelin-starred restaurants, such as Mosconi, La Cristallerie, and Fani are renowned for their innovative cuisine, impeccable service, and elegant ambiance. These establishments push the boundaries of culinary creativity, using locally sourced ingredients to craft dishes that are as visually stunning as they are delicious. Each bite is a symphony of flavors and textures, carefully curated to delight the senses and leave a lasting impression on diners.

For those seeking a more casual dining experience, Luxembourg's bistros and brasseries offer a laid-back atmosphere and a menu of classic dishes with a modern twist. Whether you're craving a hearty steak frites, a comforting bowl of Luxembourgish potato soup, or a decadent plate of seafood, you'll find plenty of options to satisfy your appetite.

Luxembourg's multicultural population has also contributed to a vibrant street food scene, with food trucks and markets offering a tantalizing array of international flavors and cuisines. From Korean BBQ to Mexican tacos to Lebanese falafel, you can take your taste buds on a culinary journey around the world without ever leaving Luxembourg.

Of course, no dining experience in Luxembourg would be complete without sampling some of the country's world-renowned wines. Luxembourg's Moselle region is famous for its crisp white wines, particularly Riesling and Pinot Blanc, which pair perfectly with the local cuisine. Many restaurants offer extensive wine lists featuring both local and international varietals, allowing diners to discover new and exciting flavors with each sip.

Beyond the dining table, Luxembourg's culinary scene is also celebrated through a variety of food festivals, culinary events, and cooking classes. From the Emaischen pottery market to the Gourmet Days food festival to the Riesling Open wine tasting event, there are plenty of opportunities to immerse yourself in Luxembourg's gastronomic culture and learn from the country's top chefs and artisans.

In essence, Luxembourg's fine dining and culinary delights are a testament to the country's passion for food, hospitality, and innovation. Whether you're indulging in a gourmet tasting menu, savoring street food from around the world, or sampling local wines in a picturesque vineyard, Luxembourg offers a dining experience that is sure to delight and inspire.

Luxembourg's Wine Country: Vineyards and Varietals

Nestled along the picturesque Moselle River, Luxembourg's wine country is a hidden gem waiting to be discovered by wine enthusiasts and travelers alike. With a winemaking tradition that dates back over a thousand years, Luxembourg boasts a rich viticultural heritage and a diverse range of vineyards and varietals.

The Moselle Valley, which stretches along the border between Luxembourg and Germany, is the heart of Luxembourg's wine country. Here, steep terraced slopes and fertile riverbanks provide the perfect conditions for growing grapes, particularly white wine varietals such as Riesling, Pinot Blanc, and Auxerrois.

Luxembourg's winegrowing regions are characterized by their unique microclimates and terroirs, which contribute to the distinctive flavors and aromas of the wines produced here. The Moselle Valley's cool climate and mineral-rich soils impart a crisp acidity and a pronounced minerality to the wines, making them ideal for pairing with a variety of dishes.

Luxembourg's winemakers take great pride in their craft, employing traditional winemaking techniques and sustainable practices to produce high-quality wines that reflect the unique characteristics of the region. Many wineries offer guided tours and tastings, allowing visitors to learn about the winemaking process firsthand and sample a selection of wines straight from the source.

In addition to its white wines, Luxembourg also produces a smaller quantity of red and rosé wines, primarily from varietals such as Pinot Noir and Gamay. These wines are known for their vibrant fruit flavors, soft tannins, and elegant structure, making them a popular choice among wine enthusiasts and connoisseurs.

Luxembourg's wine country is also home to several wine festivals and events throughout the year, including the Moselle Wine Festival in Grevenmacher and the Riesling Open in Wormeldange. These celebrations offer the perfect opportunity to sample a wide range of wines, enjoy local cuisine, and experience the warm hospitality of Luxembourg's winemaking community.

Overall, Luxembourg's wine country is a destination worth exploring for wine lovers and travelers seeking a unique and memorable experience. Whether you're strolling through vineyards overlooking the Moselle River, tasting wines in historic cellars, or enjoying a leisurely meal at a winery restaurant, Luxembourg offers a wine experience like no other.

Exploring Luxembourg's Wildlife: Forests, Rivers, and Nature Reserves

Exploring Luxembourg's wildlife is an adventure waiting to unfold, with its diverse landscapes offering a haven for a wide variety of flora and fauna. The country's lush forests, meandering rivers, and protected nature reserves provide ample opportunities for nature enthusiasts to observe and appreciate the natural world.

Luxembourg's forests cover nearly one-third of the country's total land area, making them a vital habitat for many species of plants and animals. These forests, which consist primarily of beech, oak, and pine trees, are home to deer, wild boar, foxes, and a plethora of bird species, including woodpeckers, owls, and songbirds.

The rivers and streams that crisscross Luxembourg's countryside are teeming with life, from freshwater fish and amphibians to aquatic insects and crustaceans. The Moselle River, which forms part of Luxembourg's eastern border, supports a diverse ecosystem that includes fish such as trout, perch, and pike. The Sûre and Alzette rivers, which flow through the heart of the country, are also important habitats for aquatic wildlife.

In addition to its forests and rivers, Luxembourg boasts several nature reserves and protected areas that are dedicated to preserving biodiversity and promoting conservation. The Mullerthal Region -

Luxembourg's "Little Switzerland" - is renowned for its rugged terrain, dense forests, and scenic hiking trails. The Luxembourg Ardennes, located in the north of the country, is home to dense woodlands, rolling hills, and picturesque villages, providing a tranquil retreat for both humans and wildlife alike.

Luxembourg's commitment to environmental stewardship is evident in its efforts to protect and preserve its natural heritage. The country has designated several areas as Natura 2000 sites, which are part of a network of protected areas across Europe aimed at conserving biodiversity and habitats of European significance. These sites serve as important refuges for endangered species and provide valuable habitats for wildlife to thrive.

Nature lovers visiting Luxembourg can explore its wildlife and natural landscapes through a variety of outdoor activities, including hiking, birdwatching, and wildlife photography. The country's extensive network of hiking trails offers opportunities to explore its forests, meadows, and wetlands, while its numerous nature centers and visitor centers provide educational resources and guided tours for those eager to learn more about the local flora and fauna.

In conclusion, exploring Luxembourg's wildlife is a rewarding experience that offers a glimpse into the country's natural beauty and biodiversity. From its ancient forests to its meandering rivers and protected nature reserves, Luxembourg's landscapes are teeming with life, waiting to be discovered and appreciated by nature enthusiasts of all ages.

Flora and Fauna: Biodiversity in Luxembourg

Flora and fauna flourish in the diverse landscapes of Luxembourg, creating a rich tapestry of biodiversity that is both fascinating and important for the ecosystem. The country's varied terrain, which includes forests, meadows, rivers, and wetlands, provides habitats for a wide array of plant and animal species.

In Luxembourg's forests, you'll find a mix of deciduous and coniferous trees, including beech, oak, pine, and spruce. These forests are home to numerous plant species, from wildflowers like bluebells and foxgloves to ferns, mosses, and lichens. In the spring and summer months, the forest floor bursts into life with a colorful display of blossoms and foliage, attracting insects, birds, and small mammals.

Luxembourg's rivers and streams are inhabited by a diverse range of freshwater fish, including trout, perch, pike, and grayling. These waterways also support populations of amphibians such as frogs, toads, and salamanders, as well as a variety of aquatic insects and crustaceans. Along the banks of the rivers, you'll find lush vegetation, including reeds, sedges, and water lilies, providing cover and food for wildlife.

In addition to its forests and rivers, Luxembourg is home to a number of wetlands and marshes, which are important breeding grounds and stopover sites for migratory birds. These wetlands support a variety of plant species, including cattails, bulrushes, and waterfowl such as ducks, geese, and swans. They also provide critical habitat for amphibians, reptiles, and small mammals.

Luxembourg's meadows and grasslands are another important component of the country's biodiversity, supporting a wide variety of plant and animal species. These open spaces are home to wildflowers like buttercups, daisies, and clover, as well as grasses and sedges. They provide valuable habitat for pollinators such as bees and butterflies, as well as small mammals and ground-nesting birds.

The country's agricultural landscapes also contribute to its biodiversity, with hedgerows, field margins, and fallow fields providing habitat for a variety of plant and animal species. Traditional farming practices, such as crop rotation and organic farming, help to maintain biodiversity and preserve the natural balance of the ecosystem.

Overall, Luxembourg's flora and fauna are a testament to the country's commitment to conservation and environmental stewardship. By protecting and preserving its natural habitats, Luxembourg ensures that future generations can continue to enjoy the beauty and diversity of its landscapes and wildlife.

Luxembourg's National Parks and Protected Areas

Luxembourg's commitment to environmental conservation is evident in its network of national parks and protected areas, which safeguard the country's natural heritage and promote biodiversity. While Luxembourg may be small in size, it boasts several designated areas that are dedicated to preserving its diverse landscapes and ecosystems.

One of Luxembourg's most notable protected areas is the Mullerthal Region - also known as "Little Switzerland" - located in the eastern part of the country. This picturesque region is characterized by its rugged sandstone rock formations, dense forests, and meandering streams, making it a popular destination for hiking, rock climbing, and nature exploration.

The Mullerthal Trail, a 112-kilometer-long hiking route that winds through the region, offers visitors the chance to explore its scenic beauty and discover its hidden gems. Along the way, hikers will encounter moss-covered boulders, cascading waterfalls, and enchanting woodland paths, providing a true immersion into Luxembourg's natural wonders.

In addition to the Mullerthal Region, Luxembourg is home to several other protected areas, including the Upper Sûre Natural Park and the Our Nature Park. These parks are dedicated to preserving the country's water resources, biodiversity, and cultural heritage, providing opportunities for outdoor recreation, wildlife observation, and environmental education.

The Upper Sûre Natural Park, located in the north of Luxembourg, encompasses the Upper Sûre Lake, the country's largest reservoir, as well as surrounding forests, wetlands, and meadows. The park is a haven for birdwatchers, with over 200 species of birds recorded in the area, including herons, kingfishers, and ospreys.

The Our Nature Park, situated along the border with Germany and Belgium, is characterized by its rolling hills, dense forests, and picturesque villages. The park is home to a variety of plant and animal species, including wild boar, deer, and rare orchids. Visitors can explore the park's network of hiking trails, cycle routes, and scenic viewpoints, immersing themselves in the natural beauty of the Ardennes region.

Overall, Luxembourg's national parks and protected areas are a testament to the country's commitment to conservation and sustainable development. By preserving its natural landscapes and ecosystems, Luxembourg ensures that future generations can continue to enjoy and appreciate the beauty and biodiversity of the country's natural heritage.

Discovering Luxembourg City: Landmarks and Architecture

Discovering Luxembourg City is like stepping into a living museum of history and culture, where ancient fortifications blend seamlessly with modern architecture. As the capital and largest city of the Grand Duchy of Luxembourg, Luxembourg City boasts a rich heritage that spans over a thousand years.

One of the most iconic landmarks in Luxembourg City is the UNESCO-listed Old Town, known as the "Ville Haute." Here, visitors can wander through narrow cobblestone streets lined with medieval houses, charming cafes, and artisan shops. The centerpiece of the Old Town is the Grand Ducal Palace, the official residence of the Grand Duke of Luxembourg, which dates back to the 16th century.

Perched atop a rocky promontory overlooking the Alzette River, the Bock Casemates are a testament to Luxembourg City's medieval fortifications. These underground tunnels and galleries, carved out of solid rock, once served as a strategic defense system for the city, providing shelter for soldiers and residents during times of siege.

Another must-see landmark in Luxembourg City is the imposing Notre-Dame Cathedral, a stunning example of Gothic architecture that dates back to the 17th century. The cathedral's intricate stained glass windows, towering spires, and ornate facade are a sight to behold, drawing visitors from near and far.

Luxembourg City is also home to a number of impressive museums and cultural institutions, including the National Museum of History and Art, the Mudam (Museum of Modern Art), and the Luxembourg City History Museum. These museums showcase the country's rich history, art, and cultural heritage, offering insight into Luxembourg's past and present.

In addition to its historic landmarks and cultural attractions, Luxembourg City boasts a vibrant culinary scene, with a wide variety of restaurants, cafes, and bistros serving up traditional Luxembourgish cuisine as well as international fare. Visitors can sample local specialties such as Judd mat Gaardebounen (smoked pork collar with broad beans) and Quetschentaart (plum tart) while enjoying views of the city's picturesque skyline.

Luxembourg City's modern skyline is dominated by sleek skyscrapers and contemporary architecture, a testament to the city's status as a major financial center and hub of European institutions. The Kirchberg district, located to the northeast of the city center, is home to the European Court of Justice, the European Investment Bank, and numerous other international organizations.

Overall, Luxembourg City is a fascinating blend of old and new, where ancient history meets modern innovation. Whether exploring its historic landmarks, wandering through its charming streets, or enjoying its vibrant cultural scene, visitors are sure to be captivated by the timeless beauty and charm of Luxembourg's capital city.

The Grand Ducal Palace: Symbol of Sovereignty

The Grand Ducal Palace stands as a majestic symbol of sovereignty in the heart of Luxembourg City, serving as the official residence of the Grand Duke of Luxembourg. This historic palace, with its elegant neoclassical facade and ornate interiors, is an iconic landmark that embodies the country's rich history and royal heritage.

Originally constructed in the 16th century as a city hall for the local magistrates, the Grand Ducal Palace underwent several renovations and expansions over the centuries before being transformed into the grand residence it is today. Its prime location on the Place Guillaume II, surrounded by historic buildings and bustling cafes, further enhances its prominence and significance within the cityscape.

The architecture of the Grand Ducal Palace reflects the neoclassical style popular in the 19th century, characterized by symmetrical proportions, grand columns, and elaborate decorative elements. The facade features a series of Corinthian columns, topped by a triangular pediment adorned with sculptural reliefs and the coat of arms of the Grand Duke.

While the exterior of the Grand Ducal Palace is impressive in its own right, it is the interior that truly dazzles visitors with its opulent decor and exquisite furnishings. The State Rooms, which are used for official functions and ceremonies, are adorned with chandeliers, tapestries, and works of art that reflect the grandeur and elegance of the royal court.

Visitors to the Grand Ducal Palace can explore the State Rooms and other areas of the palace during guided tours offered throughout the year. These tours provide insight into the history and significance of the palace, as well as the role of the Grand Duke and the royal family in Luxembourgian society.

In addition to its ceremonial functions, the Grand Ducal Palace also serves as a venue for important state events, such as the National Day celebrations and official receptions for visiting dignitaries. It is a symbol of national pride and identity, representing the continuity of Luxembourg's monarchy and its commitment to democratic governance.

Overall, the Grand Ducal Palace is more than just a historic building; it is a living symbol of Luxembourg's sovereignty, tradition, and cultural heritage. As one of the most recognizable landmarks in the country, it continues to inspire awe and admiration among visitors and residents alike, standing as a testament to Luxembourg's rich history and royal legacy.

Casemates du Bock: Underground Fortifications

The Casemates du Bock, located in Luxembourg City, are a remarkable network of underground fortifications that date back to the 17th century. These tunnels and galleries, carved out of solid rock beneath the Bock promontory, served as a crucial defensive system for the city, protecting it from invading forces and providing shelter for soldiers and residents during times of siege.

Originally constructed by the Spanish in the 17th century, the Casemates du Bock were expanded and reinforced by subsequent rulers, including the French and the Austrians. At their peak, the casemates stretched for over 23 kilometers and included numerous chambers, staircases, and gun emplacements, making them one of the largest underground fortifications in Europe.

The strategic location of the Casemates du Bock, perched atop a rocky plateau overlooking the Alzette River, made them virtually impregnable to enemy attacks. The tunnels were designed to withstand cannon fire and bombardment, providing a safe haven for soldiers to defend the city from within.

During times of peace, the Casemates du Bock served various purposes, including storage facilities, workshops, and even a prison for political prisoners. In the 19th century, parts of the casemates were converted into civilian housing, with families living in the underground tunnels until the early 20th century.

Today, the Casemates du Bock are a popular tourist attraction, offering visitors the chance to explore this fascinating underground world and learn about Luxembourg City's military history. Guided tours take visitors through the labyrinthine tunnels, where they can see restored chambers, original gun emplacements, and displays of historical artifacts.

Walking through the Casemates du Bock, visitors can imagine what life was like for the soldiers and residents who once inhabited these underground passages. The damp, dimly lit tunnels evoke a sense of mystery and intrigue, while the echoes of footsteps and whispered voices add to the atmosphere of the underground fortress.

In addition to their historical significance, the Casemates du Bock also offer stunning views of Luxembourg City and the surrounding countryside from their elevated vantage point. Visitors can climb to the top of the Bock promontory, where they can enjoy panoramic views of the city's skyline and the winding Alzette River below.

Overall, the Casemates du Bock are a testament to Luxembourg's military prowess and ingenuity, as well as a reminder of the city's turbulent past. They stand as a remarkable example of medieval engineering and continue to captivate visitors with their fascinating history and unique underground architecture.

Notre-Dame Cathedral: A Blend of Gothic and Renaissance Styles

The Notre-Dame Cathedral in Luxembourg City stands as a magnificent testament to the country's rich architectural heritage, blending elements of Gothic and Renaissance styles. Constructed between the 17th and 19th centuries, the cathedral is a masterpiece of design and craftsmanship, attracting visitors from around the world with its stunning facade and ornate interiors.

The cathedral's origins can be traced back to the early Middle Ages when a Romanesque church dedicated to Notre-Dame was first built on the site. Over the centuries, the church underwent several renovations and expansions, culminating in the construction of the current cathedral in the 17th century.

The architecture of the Notre-Dame Cathedral reflects the evolving tastes and influences of the time, combining Gothic and Renaissance elements to create a harmonious and visually striking structure. The facade of the cathedral features a blend of pointed arches, intricate tracery, and decorative sculptures, typical of the Gothic style, while the interior showcases elegant columns, vaulted ceilings, and Renaissance-inspired motifs.

One of the most notable features of the Notre-Dame Cathedral is its stunning stained glass windows, which depict scenes from the Bible and the lives of saints in vibrant colors and intricate details. These windows, created by renowned artists such as Jean-Baptiste Capronnier and Nicolas Becker, bathe the interior of the cathedral in a warm and ethereal light, creating a sense of awe and reverence for visitors.

The interior of the Notre-Dame Cathedral is also adorned with beautiful altars, sculptures, and paintings, many of which were commissioned by the clergy and nobility of Luxembourg. The high altar, dedicated to the Virgin Mary, is a masterpiece of Baroque artistry, featuring gilded woodwork, marble columns, and intricate carvings.

Throughout its history, the Notre-Dame Cathedral has played a central role in the religious and cultural life of Luxembourg, hosting important ceremonies, royal weddings, and state funerals. It is also a place of pilgrimage for Catholics, who come to pay their respects to the Virgin Mary and seek solace in prayer and reflection.

Today, the Notre-Dame Cathedral continues to inspire awe and admiration with its timeless beauty and spiritual significance. Whether admired from the outside for its Gothic spires and intricate carvings or explored from within for its majestic interiors and sacred atmosphere, the cathedral stands as a testament to Luxembourg's enduring faith and artistic legacy.

The Grund: Quaint Neighborhoods and Riverside Charm

Nestled along the banks of the Alzette River, the Grund is one of the most picturesque neighborhoods in Luxembourg City, known for its quaint charm and historic ambiance. This charming district, situated below the towering cliffs of the Bock promontory, has a rich history that dates back to the medieval era.

Originally a bustling commercial hub and artisan quarter, the Grund has retained much of its medieval character, with narrow cobblestone streets, half-timbered houses, and charming courtyards that evoke a sense of old-world charm. Walking through the Grund feels like stepping back in time, with its winding alleys and hidden corners revealing centuries of history and heritage.

One of the highlights of the Grund is the Neumünster Abbey, a former Benedictine monastery that dates back to the 17th century. Today, the abbey has been transformed into a cultural center and event space, hosting concerts, exhibitions, and festivals throughout the year. Its tranquil gardens and riverside terrace offer breathtaking views of the Alzette River and the surrounding countryside.

The Grund is also home to a vibrant arts and cultural scene, with numerous galleries, studios, and performance spaces showcasing the work of local and international artists. Visitors can explore the district's eclectic mix of contemporary art and traditional craftsmanship, from ceramics and textiles to painting and sculpture.

In addition to its cultural attractions, the Grund is a popular destination for outdoor enthusiasts, with scenic walking and cycling trails that wind along the riverbank and through the surrounding countryside. The Alzette Valley Trail, in particular, offers stunning views of the Grund's historic buildings and natural landscapes, making it a favorite spot for leisurely strolls and picnics.

The Grund is also known for its lively restaurant and cafe scene, with a variety of dining options ranging from cozy bistros and traditional taverns to upscale eateries and international cuisines. Visitors can sample local specialties such as Luxembourgish sausages, hearty stews, and artisanal cheeses, while enjoying the riverside ambiance and warm hospitality of the locals.

Overall, the Grund is a hidden gem waiting to be discovered by visitors to Luxembourg City, offering a perfect blend of historic charm, cultural richness, and natural beauty. Whether exploring its historic landmarks, sampling its culinary delights, or simply soaking in the riverside atmosphere, the Grund promises an unforgettable experience for travelers seeking an authentic taste of Luxembourg's heritage.

Exploring Historic Cities: Esch-sur-Alzette, Dudelange, and Echternach

Exploring historic cities in Luxembourg offers a fascinating glimpse into the country's rich cultural heritage and architectural diversity. Three cities, in particular, stand out for their unique charm and historical significance: Esch-sur-Alzette, Dudelange, and Echternach.

Esch-sur-Alzette, often referred to as the "Steel City," is Luxembourg's second-largest city and a vibrant hub of culture and industry. With its roots dating back to Roman times, Esch-sur-Alzette has a long and storied history that is reflected in its architecture and urban landscape. Visitors can explore the city's historic center, which is home to beautiful Art Nouveau buildings, quaint squares, and charming cafes. The city is also known for its cultural attractions, including the Esch-Belval district, a former industrial site that has been transformed into a modern urban quarter with museums, theaters, and concert halls.

Dudelange, located in the southwest of Luxembourg, is another city with a rich history and cultural heritage. Founded in the Middle Ages, Dudelange grew rapidly during the industrial revolution, becoming known for its steel production and mining industry. Today, the city is home to several historic landmarks, including the Château de Dudelange, a medieval fortress that has been converted into a cultural center and museum.

Dudelange also hosts a variety of cultural events and festivals throughout the year, including the Nuit des Lampions, a popular lantern festival held in the city's historic center.

Echternach, situated in the eastern part of Luxembourg, is one of the country's oldest cities and a UNESCO World Heritage Site. Known for its stunning natural beauty and rich cultural heritage, Echternach is home to the majestic Basilica of St. Willibrord, a Romanesque church dating back to the 11th century. The city is also famous for its annual Dancing Procession, a religious festival held in honor of St. Willibrord, which draws thousands of visitors from around the world. In addition to its religious significance, Echternach is a popular destination for outdoor enthusiasts, with hiking trails, cycling routes, and scenic viewpoints offering breathtaking views of the surrounding countryside.

Overall, exploring historic cities like Esch-sur-Alzette, Dudelange, and Echternach offers a unique opportunity to delve into Luxembourg's past and experience its rich cultural heritage firsthand. From medieval castles and Romanesque churches to bustling town squares and charming cobblestone streets, these cities are a treasure trove of history, culture, and architectural beauty, waiting to be discovered by visitors from near and far.

Luxembourg's Industrial Heart: Esch-sur-Alzette

Luxembourg's industrial heart beats strongest in Esch-sur-Alzette, a city rich in history and culture, yet deeply intertwined with the steel and mining industries that have shaped its identity. Situated in the southern part of the country, Esch-sur-Alzette has a long and storied history, dating back to Roman times when it was known for its iron ore deposits and strategic location along the Alzette River.

However, it wasn't until the 19th century that Esch-sur-Alzette truly began to flourish as an industrial powerhouse. The discovery of rich iron ore deposits in the region led to a boom in steel production, attracting workers from across Europe and transforming the city into the beating heart of Luxembourg's industrial revolution.

The arrival of steel magnate Émile Mayrisch in the late 19th century further fueled Esch-sur-Alzette's industrial growth, with the establishment of the ARBED steel company (later known as ArcelorMittal) cementing the city's reputation as a center of steel production. The blast furnaces and steel mills that sprang up along the banks of the Alzette River became the lifeblood of the city, providing employment for thousands of workers and fueling Luxembourg's economic prosperity.

Esch-sur-Alzette's industrial heyday reached its peak in the mid-20th century, with the city's steel mills operating at full capacity and contributing significantly to Luxembourg's GDP. However, like many industrial cities in Europe, Esch-sur-Alzette faced challenges in the latter half of the 20th century, as global economic shifts and technological advancements led to declines in the steel industry.

Despite these challenges, Esch-sur-Alzette has undergone a remarkable transformation in recent decades, diversifying its economy and revitalizing its urban landscape. The closure of many steel plants has prompted the city to embrace new industries, including technology, finance, and education, with the establishment of the University of Luxembourg and the Belval Innovation Campus breathing new life into the region.

Today, Esch-sur-Alzette is a dynamic and vibrant city that balances its industrial heritage with modern innovation and cultural vitality. Visitors can explore the remnants of its industrial past, from the blast furnaces of the Belval steelworks to the converted industrial sites that now house museums, theaters, and concert halls.

Esch-sur-Alzette's industrial legacy is not only evident in its architecture and urban landscape but also in the resilience and determination of its people. The city's transformation from a steel town to a center of innovation and creativity is a testament to the spirit of adaptation and reinvention that defines Luxembourg's industrial heart.

Dudelange: Steel, Soccer, and Cultural Heritage

Dudelange, nestled in the southwest of Luxembourg, holds a multifaceted identity that blends its industrial past with a rich cultural heritage. Known as the "Steel City," Dudelange has a history deeply rooted in steel production and mining, dating back to the 19th century. The city's steelworks and mines were once vital to Luxembourg's economy, attracting workers from far and wide and shaping the landscape of Dudelange.

The steel industry brought prosperity to Dudelange, with factories and blast furnaces dotting the skyline and providing employment for thousands of residents. The city's industrial heritage is still visible today in the remnants of old factories and industrial sites that stand as reminders of Dudelange's industrial past.

In addition to its industrial legacy, Dudelange is also known for its vibrant soccer culture. The local soccer club, F91 Dudelange, has a storied history and is one of the most successful teams in Luxembourgish football. F91 Dudelange has won numerous national titles and has represented Luxembourg in European competitions, bringing pride and excitement to the city's residents.

Beyond steel and soccer, Dudelange is a city rich in cultural heritage and artistic expression. The Château de Dudelange, a medieval fortress that has been converted into a cultural center, hosts concerts, exhibitions, and theater performances throughout the year, attracting artists and audiences from across Luxembourg and beyond. The city's annual Nuit des Lampions, or Lantern Festival, is a beloved tradition that celebrates Dudelange's cultural diversity with music, food, and lantern-lit parades through the historic city center.

Dudelange's cultural scene is further enriched by its diverse population, with residents hailing from a variety of backgrounds and ethnicities. This cultural melting pot has given rise to a thriving arts and music scene, with artists and musicians drawing inspiration from Dudelange's industrial heritage and multicultural identity.

Today, Dudelange continues to evolve and adapt to the challenges of the modern world, embracing new industries and technologies while preserving its unique heritage and traditions. The city's steel mills may no longer be as dominant as they once were, but Dudelange's spirit of resilience and innovation remains as strong as ever, ensuring that its legacy will endure for generations to come.

Echternach: Oldest City and Abbey in Luxembourg

Echternach, nestled in the eastern part of Luxembourg, holds the distinction of being the oldest city in the country, with a history that stretches back over a millennium. Founded in the 7th century by St. Willibrord, a missionary and patron saint of Luxembourg, Echternach quickly grew into an important religious and cultural center in the region.

At the heart of Echternach lies the majestic Basilica of St. Willibrord, a Romanesque church that stands as a testament to the city's religious heritage. Constructed in the 11th century, the basilica houses the tomb of St. Willibrord and is a popular destination for pilgrims and tourists alike. The basilica's ornate architecture, stunning stained glass windows, and intricate carvings make it a must-visit attraction for anyone exploring Echternach.

In addition to its religious significance, Echternach is renowned for its annual Dancing Procession, a UNESCO-listed intangible cultural heritage event that takes place on Whit Tuesday. Dating back over 500 years, the Dancing Procession is a unique blend of religious devotion and traditional folk dance, with thousands of participants joining in a solemn procession through the streets of Echternach, accompanied by music and chanting.

Echternach's historic center is a charming maze of narrow cobblestone streets, medieval buildings, and quaint squares, offering visitors a glimpse into the city's past. The Abbey of Echternach, founded by St. Willibrord in the 7th century, played a crucial role in the city's development, serving as a center of learning, art, and spirituality.

The abbey's library, one of the oldest in Europe, houses a priceless collection of manuscripts and illuminated texts, providing insight into medieval life and culture. Today, the Abbey of Echternach is a popular tourist attraction, with guided tours allowing visitors to explore its ancient crypts, chapels, and cloisters.

Surrounded by lush forests, rolling hills, and the sparkling waters of the Sauer River, Echternach is also a paradise for outdoor enthusiasts. The Müllerthal Trail, known as the "Little Switzerland" of Luxembourg, offers breathtaking hikes through picturesque landscapes of rock formations, caves, and waterfalls, making it a popular destination for nature lovers and adventure seekers.

Overall, Echternach is a city steeped in history, spirituality, and natural beauty, offering visitors a unique blend of ancient heritage and modern charm. Whether exploring its historic landmarks, participating in the Dancing Procession, or hiking through its scenic countryside, Echternach promises an unforgettable experience for travelers seeking to uncover the treasures of Luxembourg's oldest city.

Luxembourgers at Leisure: Sports and Recreation

Luxembourgers have a strong tradition of embracing sports and recreation as integral parts of their lifestyle. Despite its small size, Luxembourg boasts a diverse range of outdoor activities and sporting events that cater to people of all ages and interests.

Cycling holds a special place in the hearts of Luxembourgers, with the country's scenic landscapes and well-maintained cycling routes making it a paradise for cyclists. The Moselle Valley, Mullerthal region, and Ardennes offer challenging terrain and breathtaking scenery for both leisurely rides and competitive races. The Tour de Luxembourg, an annual cycling race that attracts top riders from around the world, is a highlight of the country's sporting calendar.

In addition to cycling, hiking is another popular pastime in Luxembourg, with hundreds of kilometers of well-marked trails crisscrossing the country's forests, hills, and valleys. The Mullerthal Trail, known as the "Little Switzerland" of Luxembourg, is a favorite destination for hikers, offering a variety of routes that lead to stunning rock formations, caves, and waterfalls.

Water sports enthusiasts also find plenty of opportunities for recreation in Luxembourg, thanks to its numerous rivers, lakes, and reservoirs. The Moselle River is a popular spot for kayaking, canoeing, and stand-up paddleboarding, while the Upper Sûre Lake offers sailing, windsurfing, and fishing.

Luxembourgers are passionate about soccer, with the sport enjoying widespread popularity across the country. Local soccer clubs, such as F91 Dudelange and FC Progrès Niederkorn, have loyal fan bases and compete in national and international leagues. The Stade de Luxembourg, the country's national soccer stadium, is a hub of activity during match days, drawing crowds of enthusiastic fans to cheer on their favorite teams.

Tennis, golf, and horseback riding are also popular leisure activities in Luxembourg, with numerous clubs and facilities catering to enthusiasts of all skill levels. The country's scenic golf courses, situated amidst rolling hills and lush greenery, provide an idyllic setting for a day on the links.

During the winter months, Luxembourg's ski resorts and cross-country ski trails attract winter sports enthusiasts from near and far. The Ardennes region, with its snow-covered slopes and forested hillsides, offers excellent opportunities for skiing, snowboarding, and snowshoeing.

Overall, Luxembourgers take great pride in their active and outdoor-oriented lifestyle, embracing sports and recreation as essential components of their well-being. Whether cycling along scenic trails, hiking through picturesque landscapes, or cheering on their favorite soccer team, Luxembourgers are passionate about staying active and enjoying the natural beauty of their country.

Hiking and Cycling Trails: Exploring the Grand Duchy

Exploring the Grand Duchy of Luxembourg offers outdoor enthusiasts a wealth of hiking and cycling trails to discover its stunning landscapes and rich natural beauty. With its diverse terrain, ranging from rolling hills and dense forests to picturesque river valleys and rocky gorges, Luxembourg is a paradise for outdoor adventurers.

The Mullerthal Trail, often referred to as the "Little Switzerland" of Luxembourg, is one of the country's most famous hiking routes. Stretching over 112 kilometers, this trail winds through the Mullerthal region, known for its dramatic rock formations, moss-covered forests, and cascading waterfalls. Hikers can explore enchanting paths that lead to hidden caves, towering cliffs, and panoramic viewpoints, offering breathtaking vistas of the surrounding countryside.

For cyclists, Luxembourg offers an extensive network of cycling trails that traverse the country's diverse landscapes. The national cycling network, comprising over 600 kilometers of designated routes, caters to cyclists of all levels, from casual riders to seasoned enthusiasts. The routes meander through charming villages, along tranquil rivers, and past historic landmarks, providing a unique way to experience the country's cultural and natural heritage.

The Moselle Valley, situated in the eastern part of Luxembourg, is a favorite destination for both hikers and cyclists. The Moselle River, flanked by rolling vineyards and picturesque villages, offers a scenic backdrop for leisurely strolls and bike rides. Visitors can explore charming towns like Remich and Grevenmacher, sample local wines at vineyards along the Moselle Wine Route, or simply soak in the peaceful ambiance of the countryside.

In the Ardennes region, located in the north of Luxembourg, outdoor enthusiasts will find rugged terrain and dense forests ideal for hiking and mountain biking. The Ardennes Cycle Route, a 160-kilometer loop that circles through the Ardennes Natural Park, takes cyclists on a journey through breathtaking landscapes, past medieval castles, and along tranquil rivers like the Our and the Sûre.

Luxembourg's commitment to sustainable tourism and conservation is evident in its well-maintained hiking and cycling trails, which are marked with clear signposts and offer amenities such as picnic areas, rest stops, and information boards. The country's compact size and efficient public transportation system make it easy for visitors to access trailheads and explore different regions of the Grand Duchy.

Whether hiking through ancient forests, cycling along scenic riverbanks, or exploring charming villages, the hiking and cycling trails of Luxembourg promise unforgettable experiences for outdoor enthusiasts seeking to immerse themselves in the natural beauty and cultural heritage of the Grand Duchy.

Winter Wonderland: Skiing and Snowboarding in Luxembourg

While Luxembourg might not be the first destination that comes to mind when thinking about skiing and snowboarding, the country still offers a winter wonderland experience for enthusiasts seeking snow-covered slopes and outdoor adventures. Despite its relatively modest size and elevation, Luxembourg's Ardennes region provides opportunities for winter sports activities during the colder months.

The Ardennes, located in the northern part of the country, features rolling hills, dense forests, and charming villages that transform into a snowy playground when winter arrives. While the terrain may not be as extensive as traditional ski resorts in neighboring countries, Luxembourg's ski areas still offer plenty of opportunities for skiing, snowboarding, and other winter activities.

Luxembourg's main ski resort is located in the Ardennes town of Wiltz, where enthusiasts can enjoy downhill skiing and snowboarding on a small but scenic slope. While not as large or challenging as those found in the Alps, the Wiltz ski area provides a family-friendly environment with gentle slopes suitable for beginners and intermediate skiers.

In addition to downhill skiing and snowboarding, the Ardennes region offers opportunities for cross-country skiing, snowshoeing, and winter hiking. The region's network of trails and forested landscapes provide an ideal setting for exploring the winter wilderness on foot or on skis, with stunning views and peaceful surroundings to enjoy along the way.

Luxembourg's compact size and efficient transportation system make it easy for visitors to access the Ardennes region from the capital city of Luxembourg City and other major towns. Whether traveling by car or public transportation, skiers and snowboarders can reach the slopes in just a short drive or train ride, making Luxembourg an accessible destination for a winter getaway.

While skiing and snowboarding may not be the primary focus of Luxembourg's tourism industry, the country's winter sports offerings provide a unique opportunity for locals and visitors alike to enjoy outdoor recreation and embrace the magic of winter in the Grand Duchy. With its picturesque landscapes, cozy villages, and friendly atmosphere, Luxembourg's winter wonderland is sure to charm anyone seeking snowy adventures in a tranquil setting.

Luxembourgeois Art and Artists

Luxembourg boasts a vibrant art scene that reflects the country's rich cultural heritage and diverse influences. While its art history may not be as well-known internationally as that of its European neighbors, Luxembourg has produced talented artists who have made significant contributions to the world of art.

One of the most celebrated figures in Luxembourgish art is Joseph Kutter, often referred to as the father of Luxembourgish painting. Kutter's work, characterized by its realism and attention to detail, captured the essence of Luxembourg's landscapes, people, and daily life. His paintings are cherished for their depictions of rural scenes, cityscapes, and portraits, providing a glimpse into the country's past and present.

Another prominent figure in Luxembourgish art is Michel Majerus, a contemporary artist known for his bold, colorful, and multimedia works. Majerus gained international recognition for his dynamic paintings, which often combined elements of pop art, graffiti, and abstraction. His playful and experimental approach to art challenged traditional conventions and pushed boundaries, earning him acclaim in the global art world.

Luxembourg's art scene is not limited to painters; the country also has a thriving community of sculptors, photographers, and multimedia artists. Works by Luxembourgish sculptors such as Lucien Wercollier and Jean-Michel Folon can be found in public spaces and private collections throughout the country and beyond.

Photography has also played a significant role in Luxembourg's artistic landscape, with photographers like Edward Steichen, whose pioneering work in the early 20th century helped elevate photography to the status of fine art. Steichen's iconic images, often focusing on landscapes, portraits, and fashion, continue to inspire photographers and artists today.

In recent years, Luxembourg has seen a surge in contemporary art galleries, museums, and cultural institutions, providing platforms for local and international artists to showcase their work. The MUDAM (Musée d'Art Moderne Grand-Duc Jean), located in Luxembourg City, is one of the country's leading contemporary art museums, featuring exhibitions and installations by artists from around the world.

Luxembourg's commitment to supporting the arts is evident in its cultural policies and initiatives, which aim to promote creativity, innovation, and cultural exchange. The country's annual Luxembourg Art Prize, established in 2015, recognizes emerging artists and provides them with opportunities for exposure and professional development.

Overall, Luxembourgeois art and artists continue to make their mark on the global stage, with their creativity, talent, and passion enriching the cultural landscape of the Grand Duchy and beyond. From traditional painters to contemporary innovators, Luxembourg's artistic community continues to inspire, provoke, and captivate audiences with its diverse and dynamic expressions of creativity.

Music and Performance Arts in Luxembourg

Luxembourg's music and performance arts scene is as diverse and vibrant as the country itself, blending influences from its neighboring countries and beyond to create a rich tapestry of cultural expression. While perhaps not as widely recognized as other European capitals, Luxembourg City has a thriving arts community that encompasses music, theater, dance, and more.

Music holds a special place in Luxembourg's cultural identity, with a long history of classical music traditions dating back centuries. The Philharmonie Luxembourg, a state-of-the-art concert hall located in the Kirchberg district, serves as the country's premier venue for classical music performances, hosting world-renowned orchestras, soloists, and conductors from around the globe. The Philharmonie's acoustically perfect auditorium and innovative programming make it a hub for musical excellence and artistic innovation.

In addition to classical music, Luxembourg has a vibrant contemporary music scene that encompasses a wide range of genres, including jazz, rock, pop, electronic, and hip-hop. Local musicians and bands regularly perform at venues throughout the country, from intimate clubs and bars to larger concert halls and outdoor festivals. The Rockhal, located in Esch-sur-Alzette, is one of Luxembourg's leading music venues, hosting concerts by international and local artists alike and serving as a focal point for the country's live music scene.

Luxembourg's cultural calendar is filled with music festivals and events that celebrate a diverse range of musical styles and traditions. The Echternach International Festival, held annually in the picturesque town of Echternach, showcases classical and contemporary music from around the world, attracting top performers and music lovers alike. The Siren's Call Music & Culture Festival, held in Luxembourg City, features a dynamic lineup of local and international artists spanning multiple genres, from indie rock and electronic music to world music and beyond.

In addition to music, Luxembourg has a thriving theater and performing arts scene that reflects the country's multicultural identity and commitment to artistic expression. The Théâtre des Capucins and the Grand Théâtre de Luxembourg, both located in Luxembourg City, are leading venues for theater, opera, dance, and multimedia performances, presenting a diverse array of productions by local and international artists.

Dance is also an integral part of Luxembourg's cultural landscape, with contemporary dance companies like the Grand Théâtre de la Ville de Luxembourg and the TROIS C-L - Centre de Création Chorégraphique Luxembourgeois showcasing innovative and boundary-pushing choreography by local and international dance artists.

Overall, Luxembourg's music and performance arts scene is a testament to the country's cultural richness and diversity, offering audiences a wealth of artistic experiences and opportunities to engage with the arts in all their forms. Whether attending a classical concert at the Philharmonie, rocking out at a live music venue, or experiencing cutting-edge theater and dance performances, visitors to Luxembourg are sure to be captivated by the country's dynamic and multifaceted cultural landscape.

Literature and Intellectual Legacy

Luxembourg's literature and intellectual legacy have been shaped by a combination of its multilingualism, its historical context, and its position within Europe. While the country may not be as well-known for its literary contributions as some of its European counterparts, it has nonetheless produced writers and thinkers who have made significant contributions to the literary world and intellectual discourse.

One of the challenges in defining Luxembourgish literature lies in the country's linguistic diversity. Luxembourgish, French, and German are the official languages, reflecting the country's historical ties to neighboring regions and its role as a crossroads of cultures. As a result, Luxembourgish literature encompasses works written in multiple languages, each contributing to the country's literary heritage in its own way.

Luxembourg's literary traditions are deeply rooted in its history and cultural identity. Folk tales, legends, and oral storytelling have long been part of Luxembourgish culture, passed down through generations and shaping the collective imagination of the people. Writers like Michel Rodange, author of the satirical epic "Renert the Fox," drew inspiration from these folk traditions, infusing their works with humor, satire, and social commentary.

In the 19th and 20th centuries, Luxembourgish literature began to flourish as writers sought to assert the country's cultural identity and assert its distinctiveness within the broader European context. Writers like Batty Weber and Nico Klopp played key roles in promoting Luxembourgish language and literature, advocating for its recognition and preservation as part of the country's cultural heritage.

The interwar period saw the emergence of literary movements such as Expressionism and Surrealism, with Luxembourgish writers like Nik Welter and Anise Koltz experimenting with new forms and styles of writing. These literary innovations reflected the social and political upheaval of the time, as writers grappled with issues of identity, alienation, and existentialism.

In the postwar period, Luxembourgish literature continued to evolve and diversify, with writers exploring themes of modernity, globalization, and multiculturalism. Contemporary authors like Jean Portante, Lambert Schlechter, and Guy Helminger have gained international acclaim for their novels, poetry, and plays, addressing issues of memory, migration, and the complexities of modern life.

In addition to its literary output, Luxembourg has a rich intellectual legacy that encompasses philosophy, political thought, and academic scholarship. Figures like Robert Schuman, one of the founding fathers of the European Union, and Edmond de la Fontaine, known as Dicks, a pioneering poet and thinker, have left indelible marks on European intellectual history.

Overall, Luxembourg's literature and intellectual legacy are a testament to the country's cultural richness, linguistic diversity, and intellectual vitality. While its literary tradition may be less well-known on the international stage, Luxembourg continues to produce writers and thinkers who contribute to the global conversation and enrich the cultural landscape of Europe and beyond.

Luxembourg's Museums and Galleries

Luxembourg's museums and galleries offer visitors a fascinating journey through the country's rich history, vibrant culture, and diverse artistic heritage. Despite its small size, Luxembourg boasts an impressive array of cultural institutions that showcase everything from ancient artifacts to contemporary art.

One of the most iconic museums in Luxembourg is the Musée National d'Histoire et d'Art (National Museum of History and Art), located in the heart of Luxembourg City. This renowned institution houses a vast collection of archaeological artifacts, historical documents, and works of art spanning centuries of Luxembourgish history. Visitors can explore exhibits on prehistoric times, Roman occupation, medieval life, and modern Luxembourg, gaining insight into the country's evolution over time.

For those interested in contemporary art, the Casino Luxembourg - Forum d'Art Contemporain is a must-visit destination. Housed in a former casino building in Luxembourg City, this cutting-edge gallery showcases innovative and thought-provoking contemporary art exhibitions by local and international artists. The Casino Luxembourg also hosts artist residencies, workshops, and events that foster creativity and dialogue within the contemporary art community.

Another highlight of Luxembourg's cultural landscape is the Mudam Luxembourg - Musée d'Art Moderne Grand-Duc Jean, a striking contemporary art museum located in the Kirchberg district of Luxembourg City. Designed by renowned architect Ieoh Ming Pei, the Mudam features a stunning collection of modern and contemporary art from around the world, including painting, sculpture, photography, video, and installation art. The museum's dynamic exhibitions and educational programs make it a hub for artistic innovation and cultural exchange.

In addition to its major museums, Luxembourg is home to numerous smaller galleries and cultural spaces that showcase local artists and emerging talents. The Rotondes, located in the Bonnevoie district of Luxembourg City, is a multifunctional cultural center that hosts exhibitions, concerts, performances, and other events throughout the year. The Rotondes also features a residency program for artists, providing them with opportunities to create and collaborate in a supportive environment.

Outside of Luxembourg City, visitors can explore a variety of museums and cultural attractions in towns and villages across the country. The Musée Rural et Artisanal in Peppange offers a glimpse into traditional rural life in Luxembourg, with exhibits on farming, crafts, and folk traditions. The Abbey of Echternach, located in the picturesque town of Echternach, houses a museum that explores the history and significance of the abbey and its role in shaping Luxembourg's cultural heritage.

Whether exploring ancient history at the National Museum of History and Art, immersing oneself in contemporary art at the Casino Luxembourg, or discovering local traditions at smaller cultural institutions, visitors to Luxembourg will find a wealth of cultural experiences awaiting them in the country's museums and galleries. With its diverse offerings and dynamic cultural landscape, Luxembourg offers something for every art lover and history enthusiast to explore and enjoy.

LuxFilmFest: Celebrating Cinema in Luxembourg

LuxFilmFest is an annual celebration of cinema in Luxembourg that has grown into one of the country's premier cultural events. Founded in 2010, the festival aims to showcase a diverse selection of international and Luxembourgish films, providing a platform for filmmakers to share their work with audiences and fostering dialogue and exchange within the film community.

Each year, LuxFilmFest presents a curated program of screenings, premieres, retrospectives, and special events that highlight the best of contemporary cinema from around the world. The festival features a wide range of genres and styles, including feature films, documentaries, shorts, and experimental works, catering to diverse tastes and interests.

LuxFilmFest is known for its emphasis on promoting cinematic excellence and artistic innovation, with a particular focus on supporting emerging filmmakers and showcasing underrepresented voices and perspectives. In addition to screening films, the festival also hosts Q&A sessions, panel discussions, masterclasses, and workshops that provide opportunities for filmmakers and audiences to engage in meaningful dialogue and exchange ideas.

One of the hallmarks of LuxFilmFest is its commitment to promoting Luxembourgish cinema and nurturing the country's film industry. The festival regularly features screenings of films made by Luxembourgish filmmakers, providing them with a platform to showcase their work to a wider audience and gain recognition both at home and abroad. LuxFilmFest also awards prizes for the best Luxembourgish film and best short film, further supporting and incentivizing local talent.

In addition to its cultural programming, LuxFilmFest plays an important role in fostering connections between filmmakers, industry professionals, and film enthusiasts from Luxembourg and beyond. The festival attracts filmmakers, actors, producers, distributors, critics, and cinephiles from around the world, creating opportunities for networking, collaboration, and cultural exchange.

Over the years, LuxFilmFest has become a highlight of Luxembourg's cultural calendar, attracting thousands of attendees and garnering attention and acclaim both nationally and internationally. The festival's commitment to celebrating the art of cinema, promoting cultural diversity, and nurturing talent has solidified its reputation as a cornerstone of Luxembourg's cultural landscape and a key player in the global film festival circuit.

Luxexpo The Box: Exhibitions and Events

Luxexpo The Box is a multifunctional exhibition and event space located in Kirchberg, Luxembourg City. It serves as a versatile venue for a wide range of events, including trade shows, conferences, concerts, and cultural exhibitions. The facility, originally known as Luxexpo, underwent significant renovations and rebranding in recent years, emerging as a modern and dynamic space that caters to diverse audiences and interests.

One of Luxexpo The Box's key features is its expansive exhibition halls, which can accommodate large-scale events and trade shows spanning various industries. These halls are equipped with state-of-the-art facilities and infrastructure, making them ideal for hosting exhibitions, product launches, and corporate events. The flexible layout of the exhibition space allows for customization and adaptation to suit the needs of different organizers and exhibitors.

In addition to its exhibition halls, Luxexpo The Box offers a range of amenities and services to enhance the event experience for attendees and participants. These include onsite catering facilities, meeting rooms, VIP lounges, and ample parking space, ensuring that events are both convenient and enjoyable for visitors.

Luxexpo The Box regularly hosts a diverse lineup of events throughout the year, catering to different interests and demographics. From industry trade shows and business conferences to cultural festivals and entertainment events, there is always something happening at Luxexpo The Box to engage and inspire audiences.

One of the highlights of Luxexpo The Box's event calendar is the annual Luxembourg International Motor Show, which showcases the latest innovations in the automotive industry and attracts car enthusiasts from across the country and beyond. The event features exhibits by leading automobile manufacturers, as well as demonstrations, test drives, and interactive experiences for visitors of all ages.

In addition to the Motor Show, Luxexpo The Box hosts a variety of other exhibitions and events, including food and wine festivals, fashion shows, art exhibitions, and live performances. The venue's central location, modern facilities, and diverse programming make it a popular destination for both local residents and visitors to Luxembourg City.

Overall, Luxexpo The Box plays a vital role in Luxembourg's cultural and economic landscape, serving as a hub for innovation, creativity, and community engagement. Whether attending a trade show, conference, or cultural event, visitors to Luxexpo The Box can expect a memorable and enriching experience that reflects the dynamic spirit of Luxembourg's capital city.

Luxembourg's Education System: Focus on Quality and Multilingualism

Luxembourg's education system is renowned for its focus on quality and multilingualism, reflecting the country's commitment to providing its citizens with a well-rounded and inclusive education. With a population that is highly diverse in terms of language and culture, Luxembourg has developed an education system that emphasizes linguistic proficiency, cultural understanding, and academic excellence.

One of the defining features of Luxembourg's education system is its multilingual approach. The country has three official languages: Luxembourgish, French, and German. From an early age, students are exposed to all three languages through a process known as trilingual education. This approach ensures that students develop fluency in multiple languages, enabling them to communicate effectively in a variety of contexts and engage with different cultures.

At the primary level, instruction is primarily conducted in Luxembourgish, with French and German introduced as subjects from the early grades. As students progress through the education system, the emphasis on multilingualism continues, with French and German becoming increasingly important components of the curriculum. By the time students reach secondary school, instruction is typically delivered in all three languages, allowing students to develop advanced proficiency in each.

In addition to the official languages, Luxembourg's education system also places a strong emphasis on English language proficiency. English is introduced as a subject in primary school and becomes a core component of the curriculum at the secondary level. Many schools also offer additional language courses in subjects such as Spanish, Italian, and Portuguese, further enhancing students' linguistic skills and cultural awareness.

Luxembourg's commitment to quality education is reflected in its rigorous academic standards and comprehensive support systems for students and teachers alike. The country consistently ranks highly in international assessments of educational performance, with students achieving above-average scores in subjects such as mathematics, science, and reading comprehension.

The education system is structured to provide students with a broad and well-rounded education that prepares them for success in both academic and professional pursuits. In addition to traditional academic subjects, the curriculum includes courses in areas such as arts, music, physical education, and citizenship education, ensuring that students develop a diverse range of skills and competencies.

Luxembourg also places a strong emphasis on inclusivity and equal access to education for all students, regardless of background or ability. The education system is designed to accommodate students with diverse learning needs, with specialized support services available to help students overcome challenges and reach their full potential.

Overall, Luxembourg's education system is a testament to the country's commitment to excellence, diversity, and inclusivity. By prioritizing multilingualism, academic rigor, and comprehensive support, Luxembourg ensures that its students are well-equipped to thrive in an increasingly globalized and interconnected world.

International Schools and Universities.

In Luxembourg, international schools and universities play a significant role in providing high-quality education to both local and expatriate communities. These institutions offer a diverse range of academic programs and curricula, catering to students from various cultural and linguistic backgrounds.

International schools in Luxembourg follow different educational systems, including the International Baccalaureate (IB), American, British, and French curricula, among others. Each school typically offers a unique educational experience tailored to the needs and preferences of its student body. Many international schools in Luxembourg are recognized for their rigorous academic standards, innovative teaching methods, and multicultural learning environments.

The International School of Luxembourg (ISL) is one of the most prominent international schools in the country, offering an IB curriculum from early childhood through high school. ISL provides a comprehensive education that emphasizes critical thinking, creativity, and global citizenship, preparing students for success in an increasingly interconnected world.

Another notable international school is St. George's International School, which offers a British-based curriculum with an emphasis on academic excellence and personal development. St. George's is known for its vibrant community, dedicated faculty, and wide range of extracurricular activities, including sports, arts, and community service.

In addition to international schools, Luxembourg is home to several renowned universities and higher education institutions that attract students from around the world. The University of Luxembourg, founded in 2003, offers a diverse range of undergraduate and graduate programs in fields such as law, economics, science, engineering, and humanities. The university is known for its cutting-edge research, interdisciplinary approach, and emphasis on innovation and entrepreneurship.

Luxembourg also hosts a number of specialized institutions, such as the Luxembourg School of Business (LSB), which offers MBA and executive education programs focused on international business and finance. The Luxembourg Institute of Science and Technology (LIST) conducts research and provides advanced training in areas such as environmental science, materials science, and information technology.

Additionally, Luxembourg is a hub for European institutions, with several EU agencies and institutions based in the country. The European Investment Bank (EIB), European Court of Justice (ECJ), and European Investment Fund (EIF) are just a few examples of organizations that contribute to

Luxembourg's reputation as a center of excellence in European affairs and international diplomacy.

Overall, international schools and universities in Luxembourg offer students a wealth of opportunities for academic and personal growth, fostering an environment of multiculturalism, innovation, and global citizenship. Whether pursuing primary education or advanced degrees, students in Luxembourg benefit from access to world-class educational institutions that prepare them for success in an increasingly competitive and interconnected world.

The Luxembourg School of Finance: A Hub for Financial Education

The Luxembourg School of Finance (LSF) stands as a premier institution, revered for its contributions to financial education and research on an international scale. Established in 2003, LSF has swiftly risen to prominence within the global financial community, gaining recognition for its innovative programs, esteemed faculty, and cutting-edge research initiatives.

Situated within the University of Luxembourg, LSF offers a comprehensive range of academic programs tailored to meet the evolving needs of the financial industry. At the undergraduate level, students can pursue degrees in finance, economics, and related fields, gaining a solid foundation in fundamental principles and practices. At the graduate level, LSF provides specialized master's programs in areas such as finance and economics, offering students the opportunity to delve deeper into their chosen field of study and develop advanced skills and expertise.

One of the hallmarks of LSF is its commitment to excellence in teaching and research. The school boasts a distinguished faculty comprised of leading experts and practitioners in the field of finance, economics, and related disciplines. These faculty members bring a wealth of real-world experience and academic insight to the classroom, providing students with valuable insights and perspectives that enhance their learning experience.

In addition to its academic programs, LSF is actively engaged in cutting-edge research that contributes to the advancement of knowledge in the field of finance. The school's faculty members are involved in a wide range of research projects spanning topics such as financial markets, corporate finance, banking, risk management, and sustainable finance. Through its research activities, LSF seeks to address key challenges facing the financial industry and provide practical solutions that benefit both practitioners and policymakers.

LSF also plays a crucial role in fostering connections between academia and industry, facilitating collaboration and knowledge exchange between students, faculty, and professionals in the financial sector. The school maintains strong partnerships with leading financial institutions, regulatory bodies, and industry associations, providing students with valuable networking opportunities, internships, and career development resources.

Furthermore, LSF is strategically located in Luxembourg, a global financial hub known for its dynamic business environment and robust regulatory framework. The school leverages its proximity to major financial institutions, including banks, investment firms, and asset managers, to provide students with firsthand exposure to the workings of the financial industry and opportunities for practical experience and professional development.

In summary, the Luxembourg School of Finance stands as a beacon of excellence in financial education, research, and industry engagement. With its innovative programs, renowned faculty, and strategic location, LSF continues to make significant contributions to the advancement of knowledge and expertise in the field of finance, shaping the future of the global financial industry for generations to come.

Social Welfare and Healthcare in Luxembourg

In Luxembourg, social welfare and healthcare are integral components of the country's commitment to ensuring the well-being of its residents. The nation boasts a comprehensive social security system that provides a wide range of benefits and services to citizens and residents alike.

The social security system in Luxembourg covers various aspects of social welfare, including healthcare, pensions, unemployment benefits, family allowances, and disability benefits. It is funded through contributions from both employers and employees, with the government also contributing to the financing of social welfare programs.

One of the cornerstones of Luxembourg's social welfare system is its healthcare system, which is recognized for its high quality and accessibility. The country has a universal healthcare system that provides coverage to all residents, regardless of their income or employment status. Access to healthcare services is facilitated through a network of public hospitals, clinics, and private healthcare providers located throughout the country.

Residents of Luxembourg are required to enroll in the national health insurance scheme, which provides coverage for a wide range of medical services, including doctor visits, hospital stays, prescription medications, and preventive care. The cost of healthcare services is typically covered by the national health insurance scheme, with patients only required to pay a small co-payment for certain services.

In addition to basic healthcare services, Luxembourg's healthcare system also offers specialized care in areas such as maternity care, mental health services, rehabilitation, and long-term care for the elderly and disabled. The government is committed to ensuring that all residents have access to timely and high-quality healthcare services, regardless of their medical needs or circumstances.

Furthermore, Luxembourg places a strong emphasis on preventive care and public health initiatives aimed at promoting healthy lifestyles and preventing disease. The government invests in programs and initiatives that encourage healthy behaviors, such as regular exercise, balanced nutrition, and smoking cessation, to reduce the burden of chronic diseases and improve overall health outcomes.

In terms of social welfare, Luxembourg provides a range of benefits and services to support individuals and families in need. This includes financial assistance for low-income households, housing assistance, childcare subsidies, and support for individuals with disabilities. The government also offers programs to help unemployed individuals find work and re-enter the workforce, as well as initiatives to promote social inclusion and integration for vulnerable populations.

Overall, Luxembourg's social welfare and healthcare systems are characterized by their universality, accessibility, and commitment to ensuring the well-being of all residents. Through its comprehensive social security system and high-quality healthcare services, Luxembourg strives to create a society where everyone has the opportunity to lead healthy, fulfilling lives.

Luxembourgers Abroad: Diaspora and Emigration

Luxembourg, despite its small size, has a significant diaspora scattered across the globe, with Luxembourgers venturing abroad for various reasons, including work, education, and personal pursuits. While the Grand Duchy of Luxembourg serves as the homeland for many, the Luxembourgish diaspora forms a vital part of the country's cultural, social, and economic fabric.

Historically, emigration from Luxembourg can be traced back to the 19th and early 20th centuries, when economic opportunities were limited, particularly in rural areas. Many Luxembourgers sought better prospects overseas, with destinations such as the United States, Canada, and South America attracting large numbers of migrants. Economic factors, such as industrialization and urbanization, drove much of this migration, as individuals sought employment opportunities in emerging industries such as mining, manufacturing, and agriculture.

The United States, in particular, became a popular destination for Luxembourgish immigrants during the late 19th and early 20th centuries. Luxembourgers settled in various regions across the country, including the Midwest and the Northeast, where they established vibrant communities and contributed to the cultural and economic landscape of their new homeland. Luxembourgish immigrants played a significant role in sectors such as mining, steel production, and agriculture, helping to fuel the growth and development of these industries.

In addition to economic factors, political and social upheavals in Europe also contributed to emigration from Luxembourg. Periods of political instability, such as the aftermath of the two World Wars, prompted some Luxembourgers to seek refuge abroad, particularly in neighboring countries such as Belgium, France, and Germany. Others chose to emigrate for personal reasons, such as education, adventure, or the pursuit of new opportunities.

Despite the historical patterns of emigration, Luxembourg's diaspora remains closely connected to its homeland, maintaining strong ties through cultural associations, social networks, and family connections. Many Luxembourgers abroad actively engage in efforts to preserve and promote Luxembourgish culture, language, and traditions, organizing events, festivals, and gatherings to celebrate their heritage and maintain a sense of belonging.

Furthermore, Luxembourg's government has taken steps to engage with the diaspora and provide support to Luxembourgers living abroad. The Ministry of Foreign Affairs and the Ministry of Family Affairs, Integration, and the Greater Region oversee initiatives aimed at supporting Luxembourgers abroad, including consular services, educational programs, and cultural exchanges.

In recent years, Luxembourg has also seen an increase in reverse migration, with some Luxembourgers returning to their homeland after spending time abroad. Factors such as economic prosperity, improved job opportunities, and a desire to reconnect with family and roots have contributed to this trend, highlighting the enduring ties between Luxembourg and its diaspora.

Overall, Luxembourgers abroad form a diverse and dynamic community that continues to play an important role in shaping the country's identity and contributing to its global presence. Whether residing in distant lands or returning to their homeland, Luxembourg's diaspora remains deeply connected to its roots, embodying the spirit of resilience, adaptability, and cultural pride that characterizes the Luxembourgish people.

Sustainability and Environmental Initiatives

Sustainability and environmental initiatives have gained significant traction in Luxembourg, reflecting the country's commitment to preserving its natural resources and reducing its ecological footprint. Despite being one of the smallest countries in Europe, Luxembourg has made considerable strides in promoting sustainability across various sectors, including energy, transportation, waste management, and conservation.

One of the key areas of focus for Luxembourg's sustainability efforts is renewable energy. The country has set ambitious targets for increasing the share of renewable energy in its overall energy mix, aiming to generate 11% of its electricity from renewable sources by 2020 and 25% by 2030. To achieve these goals, Luxembourg has invested in renewable energy infrastructure, including wind farms, solar installations, and biomass facilities, as well as promoting energy efficiency measures in buildings and transportation.

In addition to renewable energy, Luxembourg is also prioritizing sustainable transportation initiatives to reduce greenhouse gas emissions and improve air quality. The government has implemented measures to encourage the use of public transportation, cycling, and walking, including investing in public transit infrastructure, expanding bike lanes, and promoting car-sharing and electric vehicle adoption. These efforts aim to reduce traffic congestion, promote healthier lifestyles, and mitigate the environmental impact of transportation.

Waste management is another area where Luxembourg has made significant strides in promoting sustainability. The country has implemented comprehensive recycling and waste diversion programs, with ambitious targets for reducing landfill waste and increasing recycling rates. Residents are encouraged to separate their waste into different categories for recycling, composting, and incineration, with incentives and penalties in place to promote compliance. Additionally, Luxembourg has implemented policies to reduce single-use plastics and promote the use of biodegradable and recyclable materials.

Luxembourg is also actively engaged in environmental conservation efforts, with a focus on preserving its natural habitats, biodiversity, and green spaces. The country has designated several protected areas, nature reserves, and national parks to safeguard its unique ecosystems and wildlife. Conservation initiatives include habitat restoration, species reintroduction programs, and wildlife monitoring efforts to ensure the long-term sustainability of Luxembourg's natural environment.

Furthermore, Luxembourg is committed to promoting sustainable agriculture practices to reduce the environmental impact of food production and promote biodiversity conservation. The government provides support and incentives for farmers to adopt environmentally friendly farming methods, such as organic farming, agroforestry, and integrated pest management, while also promoting local and sustainable food production to reduce food miles and support local economies.

Overall, sustainability and environmental initiatives are central to Luxembourg's vision for a greener, more resilient future. Through proactive policies, investments, and partnerships, the country is working to balance economic growth with environmental protection, ensuring a sustainable and prosperous future for generations to come.

Future Challenges and Opportunities

As Luxembourg navigates the complexities of the 21st century, it faces a myriad of challenges and opportunities that will shape its future trajectory. One of the foremost challenges confronting the nation is the need to address climate change and environmental degradation. As a small, landlocked country, Luxembourg is particularly vulnerable to the impacts of climate change, including extreme weather events, rising sea levels, and disruptions to ecosystems. To mitigate these risks, Luxembourg is intensifying its efforts to reduce greenhouse gas emissions, transition to renewable energy sources, and implement adaptive measures to enhance resilience to climate-related hazards.

Furthermore, Luxembourg faces demographic challenges stemming from an aging population and low birth rates. Like many European countries, Luxembourg is experiencing a demographic shift characterized by a declining fertility rate and an increasing proportion of elderly residents. This demographic imbalance poses significant social and economic implications, including strains on healthcare and pension systems, labor shortages, and challenges in sustaining economic growth. Addressing these demographic challenges will require innovative policies and strategies to promote family-friendly policies, encourage workforce participation, and attract skilled migrants to the country.

Moreover, Luxembourg is grappling with the complexities of globalization and technological advancements, which are reshaping industries, labor markets, and societal norms. The rise of automation, artificial intelligence, and digitalization is transforming the nature of work and creating both opportunities and challenges for the labor force. Luxembourg must adapt to these technological shifts by fostering digital literacy, promoting innovation and entrepreneurship, and investing in workforce training and education to ensure that its citizens are equipped with the skills and knowledge needed to thrive in the digital economy.

Additionally, Luxembourg faces economic challenges related to its reliance on the financial services sector and its vulnerability to external shocks and global economic trends. The country's economy is highly dependent on the financial industry, which accounts for a significant portion of its GDP and employment. However, this dependence exposes Luxembourg to risks such as regulatory changes, financial market volatility, and competition from other financial centers. Diversifying the economy, promoting innovation and diversification in other sectors, and strengthening resilience to economic shocks will be critical to ensuring long-term economic sustainability and prosperity.

Despite these challenges, Luxembourg also possesses significant opportunities for growth and development. The country's strategic location in the heart of Europe, coupled with its strong infrastructure, political stability, and skilled workforce, positions it as an attractive destination for foreign investment, trade, and business development. Luxembourg's commitment to innovation, research, and development, as evidenced by initiatives such as the Luxembourg National Research Fund and the Luxembourg Space Agency, further enhances its competitive advantage in emerging sectors such as fintech, biotech, and space technology.

Moreover, Luxembourg's multicultural and multilingual society, coupled with its strong tradition of international cooperation and diplomacy, provides a solid foundation for engaging with global partners and addressing transnational challenges such as climate change, migration, and cybersecurity. By leveraging its strengths and proactively addressing its challenges, Luxembourg can seize the opportunities of the future and continue to thrive as a prosperous, inclusive, and sustainable nation.

Epilogue

In this journey through the vibrant tapestry of Luxembourg, we've explored the rich history, diverse culture, stunning landscapes, and dynamic society of this small but remarkable nation. From its ancient origins to its modern-day innovations, Luxembourg has continuously evolved, embracing change while cherishing its traditions and values.

As we conclude our exploration, it's clear that Luxembourg's story is one of resilience, adaptability, and ambition. Despite its modest size, Luxembourg punches above its weight on the global stage, serving as a beacon of stability, prosperity, and progress in the heart of Europe.

From the medieval fortresses of Luxembourg City to the rolling hills of the Ardennes, from the bustling financial district to the tranquil countryside, Luxembourg offers a kaleidoscope of experiences for visitors and residents alike. Its vibrant cities, picturesque villages, and breathtaking natural beauty captivate the imagination and leave a lasting impression on all who encounter them.

But beyond its physical attractions, Luxembourg's true essence lies in its people – a diverse tapestry of cultures, languages, and identities woven together into the fabric of a cohesive and inclusive society. Luxembourgers are known for their warmth, hospitality, and open-mindedness, welcoming newcomers with open arms and embracing diversity as a source of strength.

Looking ahead, Luxembourg faces both challenges and opportunities as it navigates the complexities of the 21st century. From addressing climate change and demographic shifts to promoting economic diversification and social inclusion, the road ahead is paved with obstacles to overcome and milestones to achieve.

Yet, amidst the uncertainties of the future, one thing remains certain – Luxembourg's unwavering commitment to progress, prosperity, and peace. As it continues to chart its course on the global stage, Luxembourg stands as a shining example of what a small nation can achieve when it dares to dream big and work together towards a common goal.

In closing, let us reflect on the journey we've embarked upon – a journey of discovery, inspiration, and appreciation for all that Luxembourg has to offer. As we bid farewell to this enchanting land, may its spirit of resilience, unity, and optimism inspire us all to reach new heights and embrace the endless possibilities that lie ahead. Luxembourg, with its rich tapestry of history and culture, will forever hold a special place in our hearts as a beacon of hope and possibility in an ever-changing world.

Made in the USA
Las Vegas, NV
19 May 2024